Scottish Jokes

Edited by Chris Findlater

LOMOND BOOKS

Compiled by RLS Ltd

Published 2007, for Lomond Books

© 2003 Waverley Books Ltd,
David Dale House,
New Lanark, ML11 9DJ

Illustrations by Jim Barker

First published in this edition 2003
Reprinted 2004, 2005, 2006, 2007

ISBN 987 1 84204 064 5

Printed and bound in Poland

POLSKABOOK

A Texan visitor to Aberdeenshire was visiting a farm to see the bulls.

"How many acres have you got?" he asked.

"Two thousand," said the farmer.

"Is that all? I can get in my car and drive all day and still not reach my boundary fence."

"I sympathise," said the farmer. "I had a car like that once."

Two little boys shouted at the minister, "Hey, mister, the Devil's deid."

"In that case," he answered, "I must pray for two fatherless bairns."

A keen Scottish rugby supporter was watching a match against England at Murrayfield. Beside him was the only empty seat in the entire stadium.

"Whose seat is that?" asked the man on the other side.

"It's my wife's."

"But why isn't she here?"

"She's dead."

"Well, why didn't you give the ticket to one of your friends?"

"They're all at the funeral."

Another minister was walking along the road when he saw two little girls playing in the dirt.

"What are you making?" he asked kindly.

"We're making a church," said one of the girls.

"How nice. And has your church got a minister?"

"There's no' enough dirt to make a minister," said the other little girl.

A man from Aberdeen came across a perfectly good crutch lying by the side of the road. He picked it up, hurried home with it and broke his wife's leg.

A Morayshire tramp had found a good wheeze to get food from farmers' wives. He knocked at the door, holding a piece of dried-up cowpat, and asked for a crust of bread to eat with it. The horrified ladies always made him throw away the cowpat and gave him a good meal. But at one house, the farmer himself answered the door. The tramp held up the cowpat and made his usual request. The farmer was shocked.

"Man, you can't eat that!" he said. "Come roond to the yaird wi' me and I'll find you a nice, hot, fresh one."

Notice on Scottish golf club wall:
    Rule No 979: A ball cannot be picked up as lost at least until it has stopped rolling.

Sir Harry Lauder was strolling in Dundee one dark night when he saw a man grubbing about on his hands and knees.

"What are you looking for?" asked the great comedian.

"My ear," said the man. "I've just been in a bit of a scrap."

"What a vicious fellow the other man must have been," said Sir Harry. "Would you know him again if you saw him?"

"I think so," was the answer. "I have his nose in my pocket."

The minister's son from a Highland village had been a bit of a teenage tearaway and a source of worry to his parents. When it was time for him to go away to university in Aberdeen, they were anxious about the effect on him of life in the city.

But he promised to reform and work hard. Regular letters came back to say how hard he was working, how many lectures he was attending, and so on. His father was so pleased that he determined to pay his son a visit to tell him how glad he was. It took him a long time to drive to Aberdeen, and it was well into the evening, and dark, when he knocked on the door of his son's lodgings. An upstairs window went up and the landlady's head poked out.

"What is it?" she asked.

"Does Willie Lamond live here?" asked the minister.

"Aye, he does. Just carry him in," replied the lady.

"I've kissed every woman in this tenement block except one," said an amorous Glaswegian to his friend, just as one of the male residents of the block was passing. The man immediately turned back, went upstairs and reported this to his wife.

"I wonder who the woman is that this rascal hasn't kissed?" he said.

"Oh," said his wife, "I suppose it'll be that stuck-up Mary Mackintosh on the third floor."

What's the difference between a wedding and a wake in Scotland?

There's one drunk less at a wake.

Two lads from the West Coast got jobs at a sawmill. On the very first morning, one called out to the other, "Hey, Donald, I've lost a finger!"

"How did you you do that?"

"I just tried it against this round, spinning thing here – damn it, there goes another one!"

How do you get a Highlander onto the roof?
Tell him that the drinks are on the house.

Two men were sitting drinking side by side at a bar in Glasgow. After Jack the barman had served them several whiskies, one suddenly turned to the other and said, "Where are you from?"

"From the Isle of Mull," replied the other.

"Is that so? So am I. This deserves a drink." And he ordered two large ones. "Where abouts on Mull?"

"From Tobermory."

"Tobermory? Me too."

"Well, that calls for a dram." And the other ordered two more large ones. "What street did you live on?"

"Harbour Street."

"This is amazing. I grew up on Harbour Street."

"Fancy, after all that, us meeting like this in the middle of Glasgow."

One of the regulars wandered into the pub.

"How are things, Jack?" he asked the barman.

"Och, the same as usual. The wife's giving trouble, the landlord's mean as ever. Oh, and the Maclean twins are plastered again."

Before the bridge to Skye was built, a ferry operated. One day a man on a bicycle came pedalling down the street of Kyle of Lochalsh in a great hurry to catch the ferry. As he came to the waterfront, he saw the vessel was ten yards from the jetty. Seeing a plank laid at an angle on a herring-box, he steered on to it, soared into the air, and was just able to grab the side of the boat. Hauling his bike over the rails, he said to a crewman,

"Phew! That was a close thing."

"Actually," said the crewman, "this ferry's on the way in."

Red Adair, the Texan oil-fire fighter, walked into a bar in Aberdeen one evening. The man next to him at the bar immediately spotted him as an American.

"I've been to the States myself," he said.

"Oh, really," said the Texan, in a tired voice.

"Oh, yes, I was in California a whole month. I went to a concert with a famous country singer called Benny Rogers, and . . ."

"Would that be Kenny Rogers?"

"Oh, yes. That's right. And he sang with a woman with a fine figure, Polly Darton."

"Do you mean Dolly Parton?"

The American's voice was terse, and the man decided it was time to change the subject.

"Have I not seen you on the TV?" he asked.

"Maybe. I'm Red Adair."

"What! Red Adair? I must have your autograph. And are you still married to Ginger Rogers?"

~~~~~~~~~~ ◎ ~~~~~~~~~~

Two lady teachers from a remote part of Scotland went on holiday to London together. Walking in the West End they saw a hot-dog stand. Feeling they ought to try everything, they each ordered a hot dog. When she received hers, Miss Macphail looked doubtfully at it and asked Miss MacAlister, "Which part of the dog did *you* get, Hughina?"

~~~~~~~~~~ ◎ ~~~~~~~~~~

**Why do pipers march when they play?
A moving target is harder to hit.**

~~~~~~~~~~ ◎ ~~~~~~~~~~

Hector and his smarter brother Hamish were building a shed. Hamish noticed that Hector was throwing away about half of the nails.

"Why are you throwing these away?" he asked.

"They're pointing the wrong way," said Hector.

Hamish thought about this for a while, then he said, "Keep them. They'll do for knocking in on the other side."

In the end Hector had to go and buy some more nails.

"How long do you want them?" asked the hardware dealer.

"Oh, I need to keep them," replied Hector.

How does a Moray ploughman have a bubble bath?

He has a plate of beans for dinner.

A performing arts group from the south went on tour in Argyll. One day, one of the actors rang his girlfriend in Glasgow.

"How's it going?" she asked.

"Terrible," he said. "Last night we had two sheep in the hall."

"What did the audience say?"

"They were the audience."

The Waverley Steps in Edinburgh are famous for their updraught of wind, even on summer days. A lady commuter, feeling her skirt swirl up as she reached the top of the steps, glared angrily at a man loitering there.

"Do you mind?" she said icily.

"Aye, I mind fine," he said, with a leer. "You had the same pair on yesterday."

A border rugby referee died and went to Heaven. At the gate he met Saint Peter who asked if he had carried out any action where principles went ahead of self-interest.

"Well," said the man, "I was reffing a game between Hawick and Jedburgh. Hawick were two points ahead, with two minutes to go. The Jed wing made a break, and passed inside to his lock. The lock was driven on by his forwards, passed out to the flanker who ducked blind and went over in the corner. However, the flanker dropped the ball before he could ground it. Since Hawick had played a better game all through, I ruled that he had dropped the ball down, not forward, and awarded the try."

"That was quite brave," said Saint Peter. "Let me just check it in the book."

He consulted his huge tome, then closed it with a snap.

"There's nothing in the book about it," he said. "When did it happen?"

"Forty-five seconds ago," said the ref.

Golf – the sport in which you shout "Fore!", shoot five, and write three.

A high-rise building was going up in central Glasgow, and three steel erectors sat on a girder having their lunch.

"Oh, no, not cream cheese and walnut again," said the first, who came from Coatbridge. "If I get the same again tomorrow, I'll jump off the girder."

The second, who came from Airdrie, opened his packet.

"Oh, no, not a Caesar salad with salami and lettuce on rye," he said. "If I get the same again tomorrow, I'll jump off too."

The third man, who came from Dufftown, opened his lunch.

"Oh, no, not another potato sandwich," he said. "If I get the same again tomorrow, I'll follow you chaps off the girder."

The next day, the Coatbridge man got cream cheese and walnut. Without delay, he jumped. The Airdrie man saw he had Caesar salad with salami and lettuce on rye. With a wild cry, he leapt into eternity. The Dufftown man then opened his lunchbox.

"Oh, no," he said. "Potato sandwiches." And he too jumped.

The foreman, who had overheard their conversation, reported what had happened, and the funerals were held together.

"If only I'd known," sobbed the wife of the Coatbridge man.

"If only he'd said," wailed the wife of the Airdrie man.

"I don't understand it at all," said the wife of the Dufftown man. "He always got his own sandwiches ready."

Hector and his smarter brother Hamish were running a ferry service to one of the Hebridean islands. One day it was particularly stormy and the boat was tossed about on the waves.

"We'll sink, we'll sink!" wailed Hector.

"Quick, then, get roond and collect the fares," shouted Hamish. "Otherwise we'll all be drooned before they've paid."

Dr Watson of Edinburgh was famous for his bedside manner and his ability to reassure patients. Calling on one of his patients one day, he said, "I have bad news and very bad news. Which would you like me to tell you first?"

The patient gulped. "Er, the bad news, Doctor."

"You have only one day left to live," said Dr Watson.

"If that's the bad news, what can the very bad news be?" gasped the patient.

"I should have told you yesterday."

Andy Macmillan, the barman, had a new customer who was very regular in his habits. Every day he would come into the pub and order three drams of whisky. He would raise each one ceremoniously and drink it down. After a while, Andy asked him why he did it that way.

"It's like this," said the man. "I have two brothers. One lives in Manitoba and the other in Queensland. We never see each other, but we have this way of drinking: we each have one for ourselves and one for each of the other two, and that way we feel we're still in touch."

But one day the man came in and ordered only two whiskies. He drank them down in the usual way and was about to go when Andy said, "I hope nothing's happened to one of your brothers."

"No, no," said the man. "They're both fine."

"But you only had the two nips," said Andy.

"Oh, I see what you mean," said the man. "The thing is, you see, I've given up drinking."

MacTavish, charged with stealing a Porsche, angrily protested his innocence, and his advocate got him acquitted. The next day, he turned up at the police station.

"I want you to run in that lawyer of mine," he said.

"But why?" said the inspector. "He got you off, didn't he?"

"Aye, but I didn't pay him, and now he's gone and took that car I stole."

The boy on the work-experience scheme was sent off with a painter. When they arrived at the place of work they parked at the back. The painter gave the lad a pot of red paint and a brush.

"I'll give you an easy job," he said. "Go round to the front and paint the porch."

In about an hour the boy returned.

"Have you finished it already?" asked the painter.

"Yes. But it's not a Porsche, it's a BMW."

A couple from the north east were watching the National Lottery results on television while they worked at the kitchen table.

"Hey, Tammas, it's our numbers!" shouted his wife. "We've won ten million pounds."

"Okay, okay, but just finish off today's begging letters," he said.

Robert the Bruce, as everybody knows, was hiding in a cave when he saw a spider swinging on its thread, trying to reach the cave wall. Several times it tried, and failed, as the fugitive king sat watching. Then, at last, it succeeded. What the official legend does not record is that it then turned to Bruce and said, in complaining tones, "I could have done it the very first time, but I just hate doing it when anyone's watching me."

Actually, the spider was taking part in a thread-swinging competition. When it finally swung to the cave wall, the other spiders angrily disqualified it.

"I saw him blowing you," said the chief judge.

Later, when Bruce and the spider had got friendly, they went to a tavern together. Bruce, in disguise, ordered a large whisky and three flies for the spider. The spider ate one fly and then decided it wasn't very hungry and wrapped the other two up in its silk thread to take away. As they were about to leave, Bruce noticed that the threads had worked loose.

"Hey," he said, "You can't go out like that. Your flies are undone."

On the train from Edinburgh to Perth, the ticket collector was having a fierce argument with a passenger who had no ticket. The passenger claimed that she was a schoolgirl entitled to a half-fare, though to the ticket collector she looked somewhat older. She had a big brown hold-all on her knees. In the end her rudeness so annoyed the official that he picked up the hold-all just as the train was going over the Forth Bridge and threatened to throw it out of the window.

"That's right!" shouted the passenger. "You men are all the same. First you refuse to believe I'm still at school, then you threaten to throw my little boy into the sea."

The only plumber in Glasgow to charge reasonable fees died and was sent to Hell by mistake. Eventually it was realised in Heaven that there was an honest plumber in the wrong place. Saint Peter telephoned on the hot line to Satan.

"Have you got an honest plumber there?"

"Yes."

"He's ours, can you send him up?"

"You can't have him."

"Why not?"

"Because he's the only one who understands air conditioning. It's really cool down here now, man."

"Send him up," shouted Saint Peter, "or we'll sue."

"You'll sue?" laughed the voice at the other end. "And where will you get hold of a lawyer?"

As a Christmas present one year, the laird gave his gamekeeper, MacPhail, a deerstalker hat with ear-flaps. MacPhail was most appreciative and always wore it with the flaps tied under his chin to keep his ears warm in the winter winds. Then one cold, windy day the laird noticed he wasn't wearing the hat.

"Where's the hat?" he asked.

"I've given up wearing it since the accident," was the reply.

"Accident? I didn't know you'd had an accident."

"A man offered me a nip of whisky, and I had the earflaps down and never heard him."

A ventriloquist was driving to a show when his car broke down near a farmhouse. He walked up to the farm to ask if he could make a telephone call to the nearest garage. When he had done so, he walked back through the farmyard with the farmer. As they passed the horse's stall, the ventriloquist said to the horse, "Hello, how are you today?"

"Fine," said the horse. "The farmer here gives me plenty of oats."

The farmer gasped, but the ventriloquist walked on, smiling. When they came to the byre, a cow was looking out.

"How are you today?" asked the ventriloquist.

"Fine", said the cow. "The farmer here makes excellent silage."

The farmer stared at the cow in amazement. They strolled on and came to a sheep-pen. The farmer suddenly turned to the ventriloquist and grasped his arm.

"Don't believe a word that sheep says. It's the biggest liar for miles around."

What do you call six weeks of rain in Fort William?
The summer holidays.

Hector and Hamish went to the pictures to see a film that had a horse race in it.

"I bet that black one will win," said Hamish.

"I bet he won't," said Hector.

The black horse won, and then Hamish admitted he'd seen the film before.

"I saw it too," said Hector. "But I thought he would never win two times in a row."

A woman with a baby in her arms got onto a bus in Dunfermline. As she put her money into the cash machine, the driver said, "That's the ugliest baby I've ever seen."

The woman was so astonished she did not react, but went and sat down. Then she said to the man sitting across the aisle, "That driver is the rudest man I've ever met."

"Tut, tut," said the man sympathetically.

"I've a good mind to go and get his name so that I can complain."

"Yes, go on, hen," said the man. "I'll hold your monkey for you while you do it."

The elderly man was reminiscing to his young grandchildren about his wartime experiences with a Scottish regiment.

"Yes," he said, "I fought in Africa, Italy and Germany. I fought with Montgomery, I fought with Wavell and I fought with Alexander."

"Couldn't you get on with anybody, Grandpa?" asked his granddaughter.

An actors' company was touring Scotland with a deeply unsuccessful play about the life of Napoleon. The worst moment came at a matinée in Perth, with only a handful of people in the theatre. The leading actor had taken to drinking, and when his colleague, dressed as the captain of *HMS Bellerophon*, said, "We are taking you to St Helena," he blurted out, "Take me anywhere you like, so long as it isn't Perth."

Bagpipes – defined as the missing link between music and noise.

The he new receptionist in a Highland hotel was very surprised when the young man in Room 8 came down late at night and gave her an extra big smile. Then he came round the desk and put his arm round her.

"Excuse me," she said. "How dare you?"

"It's in the Bible," said the young man. Then he kissed her.

"Really, that's enough," she said, struggling free.

"But it's in the Bible," repeated the young man.

"What do you mean, it's in the Bible?" she asked, indignantly.

"I'll show you," he said. He rushed up to his room and returned with the Gideon Bible. He opened it at the flyleaf where someone had written, "The receptionist's a pushover."

The MacPhindoe family from Glasgow had come up rapidly in the world and had moved out to a big new house in Bearsden. Mrs MacPhindoe decided they should go to the opera and rang up for tickets.

"Is that two tickets for Madame Butterfly?" asked the voice at the other end.

"No, no, for Mrs MacPhindoe."

Whilst they were shopping in Glasgow's finest department store, Mr MacPhindoe saw a diamond tiara.

"Will we buy you a coronet, Maggie?" he said.

"Don't be stupid," said his wife. "You know I can't play any musical instrument."

A passer-by outside a small Highland village saw a young girl struggling to drive a reluctant cow along the road.

"I've got to take it out to the bull," explained the child.

"Couldn't your father do that?" asked the passer-by.

"Oh, no," said the child. "He said it had to be the bull."

Hector and Hamish rented a boat to go out fishing on a loch. To their surprise, they both caught several big trout.

"We must come back to this place," said Hamish. "Leave a wee marker so we'll find it again."

Hector bent down and marked a big X on the boards of the boat.

"There," he said proudly.

"That's no good," shouted Hamish. "What if they give us another boat next time?"

A music lover was on his way to a concert in the Usher Hall in Edinburgh when he lost his way. Seeing a man hurrying along with a cello case, he ran up and said, "Excuse me, can you tell me how I can get to the Usher Hall?"

The other paused, glared at him for a moment, and said, "Practise, man. Practise."

Unsuccessful golfer to caddie:

"You must be the worst caddie in the entire world."

Caddie to golfer:

"That would be just too much of a coincidence."

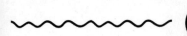

A Scots sailor was shipwrecked and washed ashore on a tropical island. As he opened his eyes and gazed around, he saw a lovely young woman wearing only a grass skirt.

"Are you hungry?" she murmured.

"Very," he groaned. She reached into a little bag woven from palm leaves and brought out a pie and chips wrapped in the previous day's *Evening News* and still hot. He ate with gusto.

"Are you thirsty?"

"Very," he groaned, more hopefully. From the little bag she produced a bottle of fine old single malt whisky, and he took a long, contented swig.

"And now," she said, nestling against him, "how would you like to play around?"

The Scotsman sat up in delighted amazement.

"Don't tell me you've got a set of golf clubs in there!" he cried.

A group of Boy Scouts from England went camping in the West Highlands. As the sun went down on the first day, the midges appeared and swarmed around, biting and tickling despite everything the lads could do to stop them. As it grew darker, some glow-worms appeared.

"It's not fair!" shouted a harassed tenderfoot. "They've got searchlight support."

Two Banffshire farmworkers were shifting a trailer-load of manure out of the farmyard. Without looking, the tractor driver swung out blithely into the roadway. A Ferrari, approaching at high speed, was forced to brake violently, swerved through the gate into the farmyard, hit a wall and burst into flames.

"Didja see that?" cried the tractor driver. "We got oota there jist in the nick o' time!"

Enjoying a round of golf with a distant acquaintance, I saw him sink a twenty-foot putt on the first green with a grunt of satisfaction. His little dog, which had come with us, promptly stood up on his back legs and uttered a shrill "Yip, yip."

"That's remarkable," I said. "What does he do if you miss your putt?"

"He turns somersaults," said my friend.

"Oh, really! How many?"

"Depends on how hard I kick him."

A Scotsman and an Englishman were in the jungle together. Suddenly, a lion appeared in the distance. The Scotsman immediately pulled off his heavy boots and started to put on a pair of trainers.

"What's the use of that?" said the Englishman. "You'll never outrun a lion."

"No, but I'll outrun you," said the Scotsman.

A man went into one of the many pubs in Rose Street, Edinburgh, and ran an eye over the huge selection of malt whiskies on display.

"I'll have a dram of that, and that, and that, and that," he said, pointing.

The barman duly set four glasses in front of him. With great speed the man drained each glass in turn.

"You were in a hurry," commented the barman.

"So would you be if you had what I have," said the man.

"Oh, what's that?" asked the barman in a sympathetic tone.

"Nae money," said the man.

When his sheepdog died, Mr McMeikle the farmer was very distressed. He went to the parish priest and said, "Father, will you do a funeral for my dog?"

"I certainly will not," said the priest. "Why don't you try the minister?"

"All right," said the farmer. "By the way, do you think a thousand pounds for his church fund would be a suitable gesture of gratitude?"

"Wait a minute," said the priest. "Why didn't you mention that the dog was a Catholic?"

On the roof above Central Station in Glasgow, a young pigeon was being educated by its parent.

"Noo, d'ye ken whit ye're supposed tae dae?" said the grown-up pigeon.

"I think so," said the little one.

"Off ye go and try oot yer style then."

The little pigeon wobbled off the ledge and flew down towards the station entrance. Selecting a man in a bowler hat, it landed with a great flapping of wings on his hat and clung on desperately despite the man's efforts to beat it off. After a while it gave up and flew back up to the roof.

"How wiz zat?" it asked.

"Terrible, terrible," said its parent. "Ye didnae listen tae a word. Watch me."

Off it flew and expertly dive-bombed a lady getting out of a taxi. Then it flew up again.

"D'ye see noo?"

"Oh, I see," said the little pigeon. "I thought ye wiz saying '*Sit* on their heids.'"

"I can never get my coffee to taste right," moaned Angus. "It's always too bitter or too sweet."

"How is that?"

"I like it with two lumps of sugar, you see."

"Well, then?"

"Well, when I'm at home, I just put the one lump in to be economical. And when I'm out, I always take the chance to put three in."

A Lewisman, planning a visit to Glasgow, telephoned the airline to ask how long the flight from Stornoway took.

"Just one second, sir," said the lady at the other end.

"Thanks very much," he said, and hung up.

Mrs MacPhindoe, of the newly rich family from Glasgow, called in an interior designer to advise on the decoration and furnishing of their big new house. As they went from room to room, he was surprised that in every room at the back of the house she opened the window, and called out, "Green sides up! Green sides up!"

Baffled by this, he finally asked, "Are you a football supporter or something?"

"Oh, no," said Mrs MacPhindoe. "It's just I've got my two nephews from Partick laying turf for me in the back garden."

Dr Watson had a patient who was both self-important and boring. One day, whilst a minor complaint was being dealt with, the patient said, "I've been invited to speak to the Rotary Club next week. The question is, what should I tell them?"

"Tell them you've got flu," said Dr Watson.

Thomas and Tillie had been married for some time and had spent a lot of it arguing and losing their tempers, with Tillie retiring upstairs and Thomas retiring to the pub. One day, prompted by a friend, Thomas went to see a marriage guidance counsellor.

"I'd need to see you together," said the counsellor, "but I will tell you one thing. A woman likes to feel loved and appreciated. Why not try telling her you love her? You'll find you feel better too."

Thomas looked rather doubtful as he left. However, during the day he resolved to try out the advice. He came straight home from work.

"How's your day been, Tillie?" he asked benevolently.

"Don't ask," she said. "There's been a power cut, the children have broken my best bowl, the cat's been sick on the bed...."

He put his arm round her.

"Never mind, Tillie, your Thomas loves you," he said.

She pushed him away with a violent shove.

"And to cap it all, you come home drunk!" she shouted.

Bring your golf ball to be re-covered. –
Advertisement in Aberdeen.

"**I**'ve given up smoking," said Angus.

"Very good," said his friend. "What was it
persuaded you?"

"It's too painful."

"Painful?"

"Aye, I've had my fingers trodden on three times
this week so far."

A schoolboy was trying on his first long trousers.

"They're too tight," he said to his mother. "Tighter than my skin."

"How can they be tighter than your skin?"

"I can sit down in my skin."

After an open-air service, the preacher passed his hat round the scanty collection of people who had stood listening to him. It came back completely empty. The preacher raised his eyebrows, surveyed the gathering, then looked skyward.

"I thank Thee, O Lord," he declared, "for the safe return of my hat."

After his barn burned down, a Buchan farmer put in an insurance claim. The agent who came round to inspect the damage and settle the claim tried to sell him some more insurance.

"Are you covered against cattle theft? And what about floods?"

"Floods, eh?" said the farmer. "That's interesting. How do you set about starting a flood?"

Camden, South Carolina, is well known as a Scottish enclave of the USA. It was there that fourteen suicides occurred on the same day. The funeral parlour had put an announcement in the window: Bargains in Coffins, Today Only.

A young couple from the Isle of Mull went to Edinburgh to be married by the registrar.

"Your name?" he asked the man.

"Donald Maclean."

"And yours?" he asked the girl.

"Shona MacLean."

"Any connection?"

Shona blushed bright red.

"Only once," she said, "and we was engaged already."

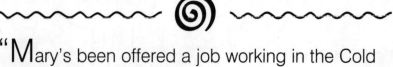

"**M**ary's been offered a job working in the Cold Store," said her mother.

"That's nice," said her friend.

"No, no, I made her turn it down. It was too cruel, poor lassie!"

"Too cruel?"

"Yes, they said she had to work in short shifts."

A famous Scottish judge was playing whist partnered by a lady of great refinement but little skill at cards. At one point the lady played quite the wrong card. The judge glowered across the table.

"Ye silly auld bitch," he muttered. Then he realised she had heard him.

"I beg your pardon, ma'am," he said. "For a moment, I mistook ye for my wife."

Why do all Scots have a sense of humour? Because it's a free gift.

After discovering they had won £15,000,000 in the Lottery, Mr and Mrs MacKemble sat down to discuss their future.

"After twenty years of washing other people's stairs," said Mrs MacKemble, "I can throw my old scrubbing brush away at last."

"Of course you can, hen," said her husband. "We can easily afford you a new one now."

A pigeon from George Square in Glasgow was boasting to one from Central Station.

"Whit's yur score rate?" it asked.

"Oh, I dinna ken. Aboot wan in three mebbe. They've tooken tae runnin' lately."

"Huh!" said the first. "Doon in George Square I hit seven oota ten, nae bother."

"That's nae great shakes," said the other. "If I had all them big-heided cooncillors strollin' in and oot o' the City Chambers, I'd get ten oota ten every time."

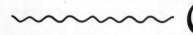

When Sanders MacGillivray came back from his first trip to London, everyone in the village was keen to find out how he had got on.

"Did you like it?"

"Oh, it was no' bad."

"As good as that, was it?"

"Well, there was just the one thing wrong. The people in my hotel just would not go to their bed. They were outside my room in the corridor shouting and banging till three o'clock in the morning."

"What did you do, Sanders?"

"Och, I just kept on playing my bagpipes."

Three Scotsmen were in jail in Arabia. One was from Edinburgh, one was from Glasgow and one was from Moray. One day the man from Edinburgh found an old brass lamp in a corner of the cell. He rubbed it and a genie appeared.

"Master, I can grant you three wishes."

"Well, there are three of us, can we have one wish each?"

"Most assuredly, O Master."

"Well, I want back to Edinburgh."

And with that, he vanished.

"And I want back to Glasgow," said the Glaswegian. He too vanished.

Only the Moray man was left. He scratched his head.

"I can't make up my mind whether to go back to my mother in Dufftown or my girlfriend in Craigellachie," he said. "I wish my pals were still here to help me decide."

And in a flash, they were.

The Highland Games were on in Blair Atholl and a man of 81 came to toss the caber.

"Don't you think you're a bit old?" said the stewards.

"Not at all, not at all. My father was coming too, but he had to go to my grandfather's wedding to be best man."

"How old is your grandfather?"

"Och, he's a hundred and twenty-four."

"Fancy a man of that age wanting to get married," said a steward.

"Och, he didna want to. He had to," said the man.

A boy aged about ten strolled into a Glasgow pub.

"I'll have a nip and a chaser," he said to the barmaid.

"You'll get me into trouble," said the barmaid.

"We'll get on to that later. First, the drinks," said the boy.

A salesman from another country was making a pitch to the furniture buyer of a Glasgow department store.

"And if you carry our new line of dining suites, I'll have the pleasure of presenting you personally with a case of fine wine," the salesman said.

"Oh, we're not allowed to accept gifts," said the buyer. "That would be a form of bribery."

"I'll tell you what," said the salesman. "Just to keep it all above board, I'll sell you the wine."

"How much for?"

"Say, a pound for the case."

"Oh, well," said the buyer, writing out the purchase order. "At that price, I'll take two cases."

An Australian entered a bar and stood beside a Scotsman.

"Where are you from, pal?" asked the Scotsman, after they'd chatted for a while.

"I'm from the finest country in the whole wide world," said the Australian.

"Are you?" said the other. "You have a damn funny accent for a Scotsman."

When Hamish left home, his mother sent him a woolly cardigan that she had knitted. "Dear son," she wrote, "to save weight and postage, I have cut the buttons off. You'll find them in a little bag in the right-hand pocket."

Hector and Hamish went into their local pub in great good humour and ordered two large whiskies.

"Are you lads celebrating something?" asked the barman.

"We certainly are," said Hector. "We've just finished a jigsaw puzzle in record time. A hundred pieces it had, and it only took us six months."

"Six months? But that's quite a long while," said the barman.

"Not at all," said Hamish. "It said on the box, three to five years."

A team of farm boys from Moray decided to climb Ben Nevis. They borrowed a van load of equipment and set off. Unfortunately, they only got about forty feet up before they ran out of scaffolding.

Two great football fanatics, Andy and Stevie, were discussing the chances of football being played in Heaven. They couldn't see how any self-respecting Heaven would not have football – but yet, they weren't quite sure. Finally they agreed that the one who died first would come back and tell the other if they played football in Heaven or not.

Not long afterwards, Andy was run over by a bus and killed. On the night after the funeral, when Stevie was asleep, a vision of Andy appeared to him. Andy was wearing a long white robe, but Stevie noticed immediately that he had football boots on.

"So they do play football there!" he exclaimed, sitting up in bed.

"Yes," said the vision. "But do you want the good news first or the bad news?"

"Oh, the good news."

"The good news is they have the most fantastic football sides here. There's more footballers here than you might think. And the angels love the game too. We play in the Heavenly League."

"Well, that's great," said Stevie. "What can the bad news be?"

"The bad news is I saw your name on the board for next Sunday's game."

A side in the local amateur league had just acquired a new player of great energy and ferocity but little else. In his first game against the team from the neighbouring town, the new player ran up against its captain, a small, balding, red-haired figure who neatly snaffled the ball from him. It happened again. And again. Losing his temper when it happened a fourth time, he muttered, "If you do that again, I'll bite your head off."

"Do that," said the other, "then you'll have more brains in your belly than you've got in your head."

Jimmy MacDaid was walking across a bridge of the Clyde when he saw a man climb up onto the parapet.

"Ah'm gonna jump," said the man.

"Oh, don't do that," said Jimmy. "Think of your family."

"I dinna have a family."

"Well, think of Rangers."

"I dinna support Rangers."

"Well, think of Celtic then."

"I dinna support Celtic either."

At this the sympathetic Glaswegian gave up.

"Jump then, ye bloody atheist!"

When Hamish was still at school, he once brought home a report which said, "We had thought Hamish had reached rock bottom. But he has started digging."

A technician was sent to Stornoway on the Isle of Lewis on a month's contract. He arrived on a grey, cloudy, drizzling day. He woke up next morning to find it was grey, cloudy, drizzling. The next day was the same, and the next. On the day after that, as he came out of his lodgings to find it was grey, cloudy and drizzling, he saw a small boy passing and said in exasperation, "Does the weather here ever change?"

"I don't know," said the child. "I'm only six."

A bank manager in rural Aberdeenshire went out to visit a farmer. When they had done their business, he was taken on a tour of the farm-yard. In a pig pen he saw a large white pig with a wooden hind leg.

"That's the bravest, most intelligent pig in the world," said the farmer.

"What happened to it?" asked the bank manager.

"Aye, weel," said the farmer, "there was a fire, ye see."

"In the yard?"

"No, no. In the hoose. The hoose went on fire one night when we were every one of us fast asleep. The pig jumped over the wall and broke in through the back door to tell us. I woke up with his feet on the bed. A brave pig!"

"Was he injured in the fire?"

"No, no. He went back inside again and dragged oot the bairns, all three of them, with his teeth."

"What a marvellous animal."

"Aye," said the farmer. "We owe our lives to that pig. There's not a finer pig in all the land."

"But how did he get the wooden leg?"

"Ach well," said the farmer, "if you have a pig of this quality, you don't eat him all at once as if he was some common animal."

When God created Scotland, He looked down on it with great satisfaction. Finally He called the Archangel Gabriel to have a look.

"Just see," said God. "This is the best yet. Splendid mountains, beautiful scenery, brave men, fine women, nice cool weather. And I've given them beautiful music and a special drink called whisky. Try some."

Gabriel took an appreciative sip.

"Excellent," he said. "But haven't you perhaps been too kind to them? Won't they be spoiled by all these things? Should there not be some drawback?"

"Just wait till you see the neighbours they're getting," said God.

A Scotsman, an Englishman and an Australian were in a bar and had just started on a new round when a fly landed in each glass of beer. The Englishman took his out on the blade of his Swiss Army knife. The Australian blew his away in a cloud of froth. The Scotsman lifted his one up carefully by the wings and held it above his glass.

"Go on, spit it oot, ye wee devil," he growled.

The pretty Sunday School teacher asked her class, "How many of you want to go to Heaven?"

They all put up a hand except Tommy Mutch.

"Don't you want to go to Heaven, Tommy?" she asked.

"I can't go, Miss," he said. "Ma said I was to come straight home or I'd get a licking."

Jim had had a bad day fishing on the river and caught nothing. On the way home, he called in at the fish shop.

"Just throw me a small salmon," he said.

"Why throw it?" asked the fishmonger.

"So that I can tell my wife I caught it."

"Wouldn't you rather have a sea trout?"

"Why would I?" asked Jim.

"Well, when your wife came in earlier, she said that's what she'd prefer you to catch when you came in."

Charlie Maclean, the life insurance salesman, had a special way of getting reluctant customers to sign on the dotted line.

"Take your time, take your time," he would say. "Don't let me hurry you. Sleep on it, and if you wake up in the morning, let me know then."

Hector and Hamish were taken on by a company putting up telegraph poles. When they came back to the depot at the end of the first day, the foreman asked how many poles they had put up.

"Two," said Hamish proudly.

"Two?" spluttered the foreman. "The other squad have put in thirty."

"Maybe," said Hector, "But I bet they left them sticking away up out of the ground."

"Are you washed yet?" said the mother to her young son, after he had been in the bath for an hour.

"Oh, Ma, there's no soap."

"Haven't you got a tongue in your head?"

"Yes, but it can't reach the back of my neck."

When Old MacPherson celebrated his 95th birthday, his cronies, for a joke, sent him round an attractive young masseuse. When she rang the doorbell, he hobbled to answer and found himself gazing at the svelte blonde figure.

"I'm here to give you super sex," she said brightly. He thought for a minute.

"I'll ha'e the soup," he said finally.

Not everyone in Kittybrewster was pleased when the bus fares into central Aberdeen went down.

"Now I need to walk into town twice instead of only once to save a pound," mourned an active elderly resident.

A visitor to Edinburgh had lunch in a restaurant and left three pence on the table as a tip. As he left, he heard the waitress murmur something. He swung round.

"What did you say?" he asked.

She replied, "I was just saying you can tell a lot about a man by the tip he leaves."

"Oh, yes? And what can you tell about me?"

"I can tell three things about you straight off."

"Tell me then," said the visitor.

"Well, you're thrifty."

"That's true enough," said the man, pleased.

"And you're a bachelor."

"Yes, that's true too. And what's the third?"

"Your father was one too," said the waitress, retreating to the kitchen.

Two robbers broke into a Glasgow lodging house. Once they were inside, a tremendous fight ensued. Bruised and bleeding, they finally emerged by the back window.

"We didnae do so bad," said one. "We came oot wi' twenty pounds."

"Aye," said the other. "But we went in wi' fifty."

The new minister came up into the pulpit with a jug of water and a glass and set them by the Bible. He was the kind of preacher who shouts and waves his arms about a lot. In the course of the sermon he drank up all the water in the jug.

"What did you think of him?" someone asked the oldest member of the congregation.

"What did I think? Miraculous, just. The first windmill driven by water that I've ever seen."

Old Angus was taken to hospital with splinters of glass in his tongue.

"How did it happen?" asked the nurse.

Angus's tongue was too full of splinters for him to explain. Helpfully, the nurse gave him a pencil and a sheet of paper. He wrote:

"I dropped a bottle of whisky on the kitchen floor."

A Scotsman was on a visit to New York and decided to get his hair cut. Seeing a barber's salon, he went in.

"How much is a haircut?" he asked.

"Haircuts start at twenty dollars," he was told.

He rubbed his chin.

"How much is a shave?"

"A shave? Oh, a shave's ten dollars."

"Shave my head then," said the visitor.

A howling baby was causing a great disturbance in the supermarket. A lady shopper saw that the child was being pushed in a trolley by a small man who kept murmuring,

"It's okay, wee Jockie, just keep quiet. It'll be all right. Don't worry, don't lose your head. Keep calm, wee Jockie, keep calm."

The lady was impressed and said, "It's a shame wee Jockie isn't being quieter when you're being so good with him."

The man looked at her indignantly.

"What do you mean?" he said. "His name is Donald. I'm wee Jockie."

Old Wattie, a notorious poacher who had recently been fined for netting salmon, had promised to reform and had even joined the church. He was walking down the street with one of the elders when they encountered the local police sergeant.

"Well, Wattie," said the sergeant, "I'm glad to see you in good company. So you're not after the salmon any more?"

"No way," said Wattie.

"Or the deer?"

"No, sir, absolutely not."

"Very good, very good, keep up the good work," said the sergeant, and went on his way. Wattie turned to his companion and heaved a great sigh of relief.

"Man!" he said. "If he'd mentioned pheasants, I would have been in a real difficult position."

One of the Edinburgh scientists who cloned a sheep decided secretly to create a duplicate of himself by cloning. He did so, but to his great surprise, his clone, though exactly like him in every other way, would only speak in the most depraved and obscene language. Not only could he not take him anywhere in public, people mistook the clone for him, and he was asked to resign from the golf club and the scientists' lunch club. In despair, he lured his clone up to Fort William. They climbed Ben Nevis and he pushed his clone off the summit to his death. Unfortunately, he was seen doing the deed and the police came for him. In vain he protested that it was his own creation he had disposed of.

"No, sir," said the policeman. "It's a serious offence. We're arresting you for making an obscene clone fall."

A visitor to the Isle of Mull lost his way in the mist and wandered about the squelching mountainside for three days. At last the mist lifted slightly and in the distance he saw a man striding along with a shepherd's crook in his hand.

"Help, help," he called.

The man waited for him to come stumbling along.

"What's the maitter?" he asked.

"I'm lost," said the visitor pitifully. "I've been lost for three days."

"Is there a reward out for ye, do you think?" asked the local.

"Oh, I shouldn't think so."

"Well, ye're still lost," said the local, and walked off into the mist.

An elderly Scottish couple had just learned that they had won £22,000,000 in the National Lottery. Overwhelmed by their luck, they discussed what to do.

"I'm going to buy the bingo hall," said the woman, "so that all the old folks can play for nothing."

"And I'll buy the chippie," said her husband. "They can all come out and get a free fish supper."

"Yes, and I'll buy the bus company," said she, "so that they can all travel home free."

Her husband suddenly stood up.

"Put your coat on, Madge," he said.

"What's the matter, John? Where are you going?" she asked.

"We'd better get round to the bingo hall. When news of this gets about there's going to be a queue a mile long and we'll never get in."

The last Hamish and Hector story: Hamish and Hector went on a parachuting course. When they went up in the plane, Hamish jumped first, pulled his cord after ten seconds and began to float down. Then Hector jumped. He pulled his cord and nothing happened. He pulled the emergency cord. Nothing happened. In a moment he over-took Hamish as he plummeted down.

"Oh," called Hamish, "so we're racing, are we?" and ripped off his own 'chute harness.

The landlord scowled at the barmaid, who had arrived late again for the evening shift.

"You should have been here at five o'clock," he said.

"Why?" she answered. "What happened?"

"That's agreed then," said Shug to his girlfriend. "We'll meet down by the bus-stop. If I get there first, I'll put a stone on top of the wall. If you get there first, take it off."

"How are you today, Isa?"

"Oh, I'm very bad, Ina, very bad."

"Oh, well, God keep you so, for fear of being worse."

"**C**heer up, man," said Mr McGonnagle to his neighbour. You look as if you didn't have a friend in the whole world."

"I haven't," said the neighbour.

"Ah, come on now," said Mr McGonnagle. "So long as you don't want to borrow money off me, I'm as good a friend as you'll find anywhere."

The blind date between Marie and Shug was not going well. He had taken the precaution of getting a telephone call half-way through the meal. When he came back from taking it, he said:

"I'm afraid I've had some bad news. My father's very sick. I have to go at once."

"That's all right," Marie said, looking relieved. "My faither was due to be deid at half past eight."

Shug was waiting at the corner of Argyle Street to meet another blind date. Every now and then he took a swig from his can of Super Lager for courage. At last he saw a pretty girl walk up and look around inquiringly. He lurched forward.

"Are you Margaret?" he asked.

"Are you Shug?" she answered.

"Yes, that's me."

"No, I'm not Margaret," she said, walking rapidly on.

Mrs Campbell: "Is your son finished learning the pipes?"

Mrs MacDonald: "No, but the neighbours are making threats."

Horse buyer: Is this horse for sale?

Seller: Aye, that's why he's here.

Buyer: How much?

Seller: Fifty pounds.

Buyer: Hmmm. Has he any faults.

Seller: He only has two faults, to be honest.

Buyer: What are they?

Seller: I'll tell what I'll do – I'll tell you the one fault now, and the other when you've paid your money.

Buyer: Well then, tell me the first fault.

Seller: When he's loose in the field he's a devil to catch.

Buyer: Oh, that's not so bad. I'll take him. Here's your money. And now, what's the second fault he's got?

Seller: When you've caught him, he's no good for anything.

A minister used to preaching fiery sermons, got really carried away one day when he described the sinfulness of his parishioners.

"Not one of you is fit to clean the midden," he shouted at one point.

This so annoyed some of the congregation that they complained to the Kirk. The minister was told he had gone too far and should apologise.

Next Sunday he ascended the pulpit again.

"Last Sunday I told you that none of you was fit to clean the midden. Well, I take it all back. Each and every one of you is fit to clean the midden."

The journey from Edinburgh to London is a long one, and the train was running late, as always. Just before it reached the big smoke, the ticket inspector checked the tickets of an Edinburgh lady and her son.

"This boy looks too old to be travelling on a half-fare," he said.

"Well he was young enough before we started," replied the mother.

A lady approached a taxi driver in Sauchiehall Street, Glasgow.

"What is the shortest way to Queen Street Station?" she asked.

He pointed to the door of his cab.

"In there, Mrs," he said.

A fight was going on between two men in front of a group. At last, one gave in. But the other kept on hitting him, ignoring his cries for mercy.

"Hey!" called one of the watchers, "can you no' hear? He's had enough."

"Aye," grunted the aggressor, "but he's that big a liar, I don't believe wan word he tells me."

A minister, visiting a town he did not know, stopped a boy in the street to inquire the way to the church. Instead of giving the lad a tip, he said:

"Remember to say your prayers, my boy, and you'll find the way to heaven."

The boy replied:

"What do you know about the way to heaven if you don't even know the way to the kirk?"

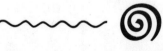

Two men working away from home were sharing a room. One day they came by a bottle of whisky, and shared it that evening, glass by glass. They resolved to leave some over for the next day, put the bottle in the wardrobe, and went to bed. In the dead of night, one was wakened by stumbling and banging.

"What are you looking for?" he said.

"Nothing," was the answer.

"Well, if you're looking for nothing, you'll find it in the bottle," he said, and went back to sleep.

"Don't worry, Shug," said his friend as Shug prepared to leave to go to court over the matter of a stramash in a Glasgow pub, "you'll get justice."

"That's just what I'm afraid of," said Shug.

Jim Barker

A bad-tempered diner summoned a waitress for the seventh or eighth time.

"Do you call this pig?" he asked, pointing the contents of his fork at her.

"At which end of the fork, sir?" she asked.

"That Private McClintock is a fine shot with a rifle," observed the sergeant.

"Yes," said the lieutenant, "but I wonder what line he was in before he joined the army."

"Why is that, sir?"

"It's the way he takes out his handkerchief and wipes his fingerprints off the gun every time he takes a shot."

Hearing of the death of an old enemy, a man commented: "Well, the devil has got him at last."

"Isn't that a bit heartless?" protested the man who'd brought the news.

"Well, if the devil hasn't got him, all I can say is, what's the point of having a devil at all?"

At the age of eighty-five, Archie McCluckie got married to a young woman of twenty-six. His doctor felt obliged to warn him:

"Be careful, now. Sex at your age can sometimes be fatal."

"Oh, well, if the worst comes to the worst, I can always find another wife," said Archie.

Intending tourist: "I'm planning a trip to Scotland in August. What sort of clothes should I be taking?"

Lady in travel agent's: "All of them."

During a Sherrif court hearing, two lawyers got into a fierce argument over a point of law. Neither would give way. At last one lost his temper completely and shouted: "You are the biggest fool I ever met in my life."

"I could say the same about you," replied the other.

"Order, gentlemen, order," interposed the Sherrif. "You seem to forget that I am present."

A man arrested for murder got his friends to bribe one of the jury. In return for the bribe, the juryman would hold out for a verdict of manslaughter.

The jury was out for a nerve-rackingly long time, but at last returned a verdict of manslaughter. The prisoner received a cautionary sentence and was soon out. When later he met the bent juror, he said:

"I'm very grateful to you. It seems you had a terrible job persuading them."

"It was terrible all right," said the juror, "there they were, all eleven of them wanting to acquit you. I had to argue like hell for manslaughter."

An old gentleman lived in a fine old house in Helensburgh. The mansion was riddled with mice, but he didn't mind. He had a favourite mouse and when he whistled, it came out and he gave it a drop of whisky.

One day, when the old fellow had a visitor in the house, the mouse got drunk, waved its paw in the air and shouted:

"Bring in the cat, and I'll fight it."

"How extraordinary!" said the visitor.

"It is queer," said the old man. "He usually fights the dog."

Mr Mackay was surprised and indignant to read his own obituary in the paper one morning. He went to the telephone to call his solicitor, Mr McAndrew.

"Did you see the *Herald* today?" he asked. "They have my obituary in it."

"I did see it," said McAndrew. "Er, where is it you're calling from?"

The editor of an Aberdeen newspaper found it very difficult to get on with his job because of the number of callers. At last he instructed the office boy not to let anyone up to his office.

"But when I say you're out, they don't believe me," said the boy. "They say they know you're in there, and they have to see you."

"Tell them that's what they all say," said the

editor. "It won't wash. I must have peace and quiet."

That afternoon, a lady came to see the editor. The office boy told her it was impossible; the editor was seeing nobody.

"But I'm his wife," she said.

"That's what they all say," said the boy.

In the Horseshoe Bar, three men were arguing over what was the oldest profession – for men, anyway.

"Eve was detached from Adam," said the surgeon. "That's surgery. You can't beat that."

"Oh yes," said the architect. "Before man even existed, order was created from chaos. That's architecture."

"And where d'you think the chaos came from?" asked the politician.

A man was fishing by the banks of the River Findhorn one afternoon. He was having no luck at all. At last he dropped the rod and looked round in desperation, just as tiny, ugly little woman came along the path.

"Are you having no luck?" she asked.

"None at all."

"Well," she said, "I am one of the Sidhe, the faery people. To make it a lucky day, I will grant you three wishes. What would you like for the first one?"

"A fine big salmon," he said.

"Noted," said she. "And the second wish?"

"A bottle of the best whisky."

"I've noted that one too, and now, the third."

"I want to be irresistible to women."

"Right," she said. "Now, before your wishes are granted, there is just one thing. You have to embrace me and give me a big kiss."

The man was most reluctant, as she was such a repulsive-looking old thing, but he summoned up his resolve, put his arms round her, and kissed her enthusiastically. At last he let go.

"How old are you?" she asked, smacking her lips.

"Forty," said the man.

"That's a bit old to be believing in faeries," she said, walking off.

At the Barras market in Glasgow, a newcomer to the city backed his car into a fruit stall. Hearing the loud altercation that followed, a policeman hurried up.

"What's going on here?" he said to the driver. "I'll have to take your name."

"It's Donald Campbell," said the driver.

"Is that so?" said the policeman. "I'm a Campbell myself. And where are you from?"

"Kilmarnock," said the driver.

"No!" said the policeman. "It's where my father lives. We'll have a blether in a minute about the old place. But first, wait till I sort out this numpty here who pushed his stall into your car."

At Customs in Glasgow Airport, a little old lady was asked if she had anything to declare.

"No, no, nothing at all." she said.

"What is in that big bottle?" asked the customs officer.

"It's a bottle of holy water from Lourdes," said the old lady.

"Will you just take the top off, so that I can take a sniff," said the customs offi-cer. Somewhat unwillingly, the old lady did so.

"But this is whisky," said the officer.

"Praise the Lord," cried the old lady. "A miracle!"

Murdoch was a smart man, always on the lookout for an opportunity. But like everyone else, he died in the end. Reporting to the gate of heaven, he saluted St Peter.

"It's a long time you've been at this job, by all acounts," he said.

"Here," said St Peter, "a million years passes as a minute. And a million pounds is the same as a penny."

"Is that so?" said Murdoch. "Would you lend me a penny then, for the truth is I've come up with nothing at all in my pockets."

"Certainly," said St Peter. "Just wait one minute."

A man came into the barber's shop, steering a not altogether willing small boy. Placing the boy in one of the waiting-chairs, he sat himself down and ordered the full works – shave,

haircut, scalp massage. Via the mirror he kept an eye on the boy, and each time the lad showed any sign of moving, he said sternly, "Stay there, now."

When he was finished, he stood up and motioned the boy into the barber's chair.

"I'll be right back," he said to the barber. "There's just something I have to get in the shop next door."

The barber got on with the boy's haircut, but the man did not reappear. When the haircut was complete, the barber said:

"You dad's being a long time."

"He's not my dad," said the boy.

"Who is he then?" asked the barber.

"He's just a man who came up to me and said, 'Hey, d'you want a free haircut?'"

Two men, arrested for being drunk and disorderly, were having their details noted at the police station.

"Name?" asked the officer of one.

"James McCleish."

"Address?"

"No fixed abode," said the man craftily.

"And you?" the officer asked the other.

"David McClean."

"Address?"

"I live just just next door to him," said the man.

Mr and Mrs McNish had got fed up with their house in Troon. The draughty sea air came in; the kitchen was too small, the garden was damp and grew fungus and mildew, the fire smoked, the floors creaked, a neighbour's shed blocked off the sea view. They put it in the hands of an estate agent and told him to sell it for them. In due course he sent them the particulars.

"Enchanting house for sale," it read. "Invigorating sea air; easy-access bijou kitchen; character features including original wood floors and fine, traditional Scottish fire-place. Sheltered from ocean gales. Fairy plants in garden. Come early to snatch up this most desirable residence."

"Mary," declared the husband. "We're not moving. I never realised what a fine house we were living in till now."

An inexperienced piper took time off from his playing to say to a guest:

"I understand you love the music of the pipes?"

"Yes," said the guest, "but never mind, keep on playing."

Feeling a sudden onslaught of thirst, and find-
ing himself in a somewhat scruffy part of town,
a businessman entered a down-at-heel pub
and ordered a drink at the bar. Next to him was
a disreputable character, with one elbow
propped on the bar, examining something
between his finger and thumb. Seeing the newcomer looking, the man said:

"Looks like plastic, feels like rubber."

"What is it?" asked the businessman.

"Take a feel," said the man, proffering the little
blob of material.

The businessman squeezed it between his fingers, eyed it, sniffed it, and said:

"Beats me. What can it be?"

"Snot," said the scruffy man.

The whole staff were assembled in the canteen for a pep-talk from the boss.

"Looking about me," he said, "I see a number of faces that aren't there. Absenteeism will not be tolerated, and I hope that those not here today will pay special attention to my words and make sure that their time-keeping is better in future."

Lady in Butcher's Shop: "What's the cheapest meat you have?"

Butcher: "Whale meat, madam."

Lady: "How much?"

Butcher: "Twenty pence a pound."

Lady: "Well give me a quarter-pound – and could you throw in the head, for my cat."

Donald: "Shall we try a different position tonight, Ina?"

Davina: "Yes, good idea. You stand up and do the ironing, and I'll sit on the sofa and fart."

The day before a Scotland–England game, the English football side booked in to a big Glasgow hotel. They all came down to dinner together, the coach placing himself at the head of the table. He beckoned to the waiter and said:

"I'll have a 12-oz fillet steak, medium rare."

"And the vegetables, sir?" asked the waiter.

The coach waved an expansive hand.

"Oh, they'll all have the same."

A man in jail for a robbery was visited by his wife.

"This is the time of year I'd be planting potatoes in the allotment," he said.

"Well, I have no time to dig up the allotment," replied his wife.

"Don't you worry about that," he said. "All you have to do is plant them. You'll see."

After she had gone, he wrote her a letter: "Dear Mary, There is some stuff buried in the allotment that should be passed on to the boys. Can you see to it for me? Love, Michael."

The following day, a posse of policemen descended on the allotment with spades, dug it all over, found nothing, and drove away.

The day after that, she planted the potatoes.

A man sitting in a London coffee house was busy writing a letter. A Scottish visitor, out of curiosity, peered over his shoulder to see what he was writing. Seeing the onlooker out of the corner of his eye, the irritated writer completed the letter by writing:

"Must end now. A damn nosy Scotsman is snooping over my shoulder."

"How dare you?" shouted the Scotsman. "I wasn't looking at all."

"When you go in there," said the temperance crusader outside the pub, "Satan goes with you."

"Well, he'll have to buy his own drink," replied the drinker.

"I'll have a whisky," said the American visitor to a Scottish seaside village. "On the rocks."

"You can take it out on the rocks if you like," said the girl in the bar, "but mind you bring the glass back."

"What d'you mean?" said the American. "On the rocks – I want ice with it."

"This isn't the season for ice," said the girl. "You'll have to come back in January."

Jimmy had had a good few drinks in the pub. What one might describe as a bucket. At last, when he ordered another, the barman said:

"I'm sorry, sir, I think you've had enough. I can't serve you."

Jimmy went out of the pub in disgust, went along the street, up an alley and back in again through

the pub's side door. At the bar he ordered a whisky.

"Sorry, pal," said the barman, I can't serve you."

Jimmy stumbled forth again. This time he left the pub, turned the other way, walked round the corner and came by a door that led on to another street.

"I'll have a whisky," he said to the barman.

"Look, pal," said the barman, "I've had enough of you. Clear out or I'll throw you out."

"Whass goin' on?" said Jimmy. "How come you work in every damn pub in the place?"

A young journalist was sent along to report on a speech to be given by a prominent politician. The speech was an after-dinner one, and it was clear that the politician had consumed a great deal of wine at the table. When he rose to speak, he was barely audible, and what could be heard did not make much sense. The journalist was left with almost nothing to say. Since his newspaper supported the great man's party, he could certainly not give a true report. Next morning he went round to the hotel where the politician was staying, and asked to see him. He explained that he had failed to take down all the speech, and asked for a copy. The politician winked at him:

"Had a glass or two too many, did you?"

"Something like that," said the young man.

Obligingly, the politician gave him a transcript of the speech as it was meant to be. As the journalist left, he placed a paternal hand on his shoulder.

A word of advice," he murmured. "You'll never get on if you let drink interfere with your work."

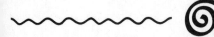

Customer: What's this slop you've served up?

Dinner lady: It's bean casserole.

Customer: I don't care what it's been. What is it now?

An elderly Aberdeen man felt ill one winter and the doctor prescribed him some medicine. In the end, however, he felt better anyway, and did not take it. The following winter his wife was taken ill. Despite the fact that her symptoms were quite different, he gave her some of the medicine, whereupon she died. A friend called to sympathise:

"It must be a great loss," he said, "especially as you have no children to help you bear it."

"Aye, but it could have been worse," said the man. "It was only by the Lord's mercy that I took none of that medicine mysel'."

One drink – is very nice.
Two drinks – is one too many
Three drinks – is not half enough.

A local laird, who had been far from popular, died, and was buried on a very stormy day. One of those who had attended the interment was describing it to a friend a few days later.

"I've never seen rain like it," he said. "We had to let the coffin down into two feet of water."

"Ah, well," said the other, "where he's gone to he'll need a' the watter he can get."

A smart gent found himself sitting in the train next to a scruffy looking woman with a little boy who kept on sniffing and wiping his nose on the sleeve of his jersey. At last the gent said, "Excuse me, but doesn't that boy have a handkerchief?"

"What if he does?" said the woman, "ye needn't think he's lending it to you."

"**H**ow was your evening with Dennis next door?"

"Fine, fine. But the man's a terrible drinker. He sat there all evening, nipping away from a bottle of whisky, till in the end I could hardly see him."

Jimmy: "Do you know what's the difference between yourself and a vending machine?"

Johnnie: "No?"

Jimmie: "You can get a drink out of a vending machine."

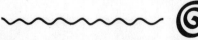

A customer in a pub stood contemplating the pint he had just been poured.

"How many barrels do you sell a week?" he inquired of the landlord, at last.

"About ten, I think," said the landlord.

"I could tell you a way to sell eleven," remarked the man.

"Oh, what is it?"

"Fill the damn glasses up."

"McLatchie is a really well brought up young chap."

"How can you tell?"

"He always gets up out of the bath to pee in the sink."

It was a stormy night as the village policeman was doing his rounds, just as the pubs were shutting. He was surprised to see Mr MacArdle standing outside his front door, making no effort to go in.

"You'd better go inside, Mr MacArdle," he said. "It's stormy out here."

"Shtormy?" said the other. "It's nothing to the shtorm thash going to break when I go inside."

Two farm lads were out driving in their pick-up truck when the brakes failed on a hill.

"Help!" cried one, "we're going to crash."

"It's all right," said the other. "There's a stop sign at the bottom."

"It's an awful thing the drink," exclaimed an indignant customer, when the barber, with watery eyes and a shaky hand, had drawn blood for the third time.

"Aye," agreed the barber. "It makes the skin awfy tender."

A Glasgow man left his almost-full glass of beer to visit the gents. Before doing so he wrote a little note saying: "This drink belongs to the Springburn Amateur Heavyweight Boxing Champion."

When he returned, the glass was empty. Added to his note were these words:

"This drink is now inside the Springburn Four Hundred Metres Running Champion."

"Why did you come here, anyway?" a Londoner asked Rory MacAllister, the unsuccessful busker from Aberdeen, who specialised in sheep impressions.

"To raise the average IQ in both Scotland and England," he replied.

A man walked into a pub and ordered a large whisky. The barman poured it, the man sat down, read his newspaper, and let the drink stand. After about fifteen minutes he ordered another.

"But you still have one standing there," the barman pointed out.

"Oh, I always hate the taste of the first drink," explained the customer.

A London-dwelling Scotsman met a friend one day, who noticed his long face.

"What's the matter, Wullie?"

"Well, I was on jury service, and I was given three days in jail."

"For being on a jury? How did that happen?"

"The judge said 'What is your name?' and I said 'William Wallace MacDiarmid MacGregor.' He said 'Are you Scottish, by any chance?' and I said 'Are you a bloody comedian?' "

After five years working for old MacMeinne in Pitlochry, the office cleaner thought it was time to ask for more pay. But when she suggested it, he looked at her in amazement:

"Are you trying to take a rise out of me?" he asked.

"I'm appealing for help for a poor family living under threat of eviction," said the man to a jolly group in the pub. "Please give generously. They need to pay a hundred and fifty pounds back rental to avoid being thrown out on to the street. They have five children under ten, and another on the way. And it'll soon be Christmas."

Moved by his appeal, they shelled out generously.

"Are you their social worker?" asked one of the group.

"No, no," said the man, "I'm their landlord."

MacCrindle and MacCracken had been partners in business for years. But MacCrindle was suddenly taken seriously ill and was given only a few days to live. MacCracken came to see him on his deathbed.

"I have a confession to make to you," whispered MacCrindle. "Remember that year when the company lost half a million, and you had to sell your house? I embezzled it."

"That's all right, I forgive you," said MacCracken.

"And I've been having an affair with your wife for years."

"I forgive you that too."

"And the time someone informed on you to the Revenue –"

"That's all right. I know it was you, but I forgive you."

"You're very forgiving; I don't deserve it," sobbed MacCrindle.

"It's all OK, now. In fact, I need to ask your forgiveness, too."

"What for?"

"For poisoning you."

The secretary of a vigorous and uninhibited businessman at last got tired of all the "overtime" he put in on her, and found herself a new job. Going into his office, she said:

"I have found a new and better position."

"Lock the door," he said. "We'll try it now."

You know you're a ned if:

Your toilet paper has numbered pages.

You hammer beer bottle tops in door-frames for decoration.

You and your dog walk down to the green for the same reason.

Your girlfriend's tattoos cover more of her than her clothes do.

You have lost at least one tooth opening a beer bottle.

There is a car without wheels at the side of your house.

Your spring-cleaning is carried out by a council squad wearing masks.

You got married in a white track suit and a baseball cap, and the bride's ring was sovereign one.

You can open a locked car faster than you can open your own door with a key.

An enthusiastic golfer who spent every spare moment on the links came home for supper with his wife and son one evening.

"Jimmy tells me he caddied for you this afternoon," said his wife.

The golfer looked closely at the lad.

"Do you know," he said. "I was sure I'd seen him somewhere before."

Golfer: "My game isn't what it used to be."
Caddie: "Oh aye, what did your game use to be?"

At the golf course at St Andrews, a caddie had been toting clubs round all eighteen holes, on a cold and windy afternoon, for an extremely rich golfer who was about forty-seven above par and extremely bad-tempered. He consoled himself by the thought of a warming drink in the clubhouse at the end of the round.

Sure enough, after the final putt had at last been sunk, he heard the words:

"Take this for a hot whisky and lemon."

Something was pressed into his hand, and he found himself holding a sugar-lump.

"Now, sir," said the golf pro. "Take the club like this, and just go through the motions without hitting the ball."

"But that's exactly the problem I'm trying to overcome," protested the golfer.

"Now, just to check your knowledge of place-names, can you spell Stirling for me," said the interviewer.

"Do you mean the town or the region?" asked the typist.

A party of accountants from a well-known international consultancy went for an afternoon's walking in the Highlands. After a while the mist came down, and they wandered off the path. When the mist lifted again, they found themselves on top of a high, steep ridge.

"Where are we?" they asked, crowding round the one who had the map.

He gazed intently at it. At last he spoke.

"See that mountain over there?"

"Yes?"

"According to the map, we're on top of it."

Another establishment close by offered heavenly views. It turned out to be a room with a skylight.

Two men got talking at a Hamilton race meeting.

"I had the most amazing coincidence here, exactly five years ago," said one. "It was the fifth of May, at five o'clock, the fifth race of the day, and I backed the fifth horse, at five to one."

"Jings, how much did you win?"

"Nothing. It came in fifth."

The ink was scarcely dry on the insurance agreement when the farmer said:

"So, just remind me, what would I get if my steading were to burn down tonight and all the tractors and equipment were lost?"

"About ten years in Barlinnie," replied the insurance agent.

The director had just finished interviewing a potential new secretary.

"That seems quite satisfactory, Miss Robertson. And what sort of salary would you be looking for?"

"About ten thousand," said Miss Robertson.

"You can have that, with pleasure," he said.

"Hold on a minute," said Miss Robertson, "if it's with pleasure, it's fifteen thousand."

Two fishermen were out on the loch one Sunday morning. As they sat with their rods, the distant sound of church bells came floating on the still air.

"Hear that?" said one. "We really ought to be in church."

"Oh, I couldn't go today anyway," said the other. "My wife is ill in bed."

"And have you any special talents, Miss Hannay?" asked the interviewer.

"Well, I'm very good at cross-words," said the job applicant. "I've won several prizes. And I also won a prize in a story-writing competition."

"Very good," said the interviewer. "But how about things that can be done in the office?"

"Oh, but I did these in the office," said the applicant.

"Your brochure said the room had a sea view," protested the hotel guest.

"Och," said the hotel keeper, "that damn post-card of Saltcoats keeps falling off the wardrobe door."

Mr McLetchie was very wealthy and his only child, a daughter, was the apple of his eye. Like most wealthy men, he wanted his daughter to marry a rich husband, preferably with a castle, and was not at all pleased when she announced that she wanted to marry a penniless divinity student. When she brought the young man home, he was subjected to an intensive grilling.

"How much do you earn?"

"Practically nothing, sir."

"What are your prospects?"

"They are in God's hands, sir."

"But how will you maintain my daughter?"

"God will provide."

"Suppose you have children – who's going to clothe and feed them?"

"God will take care of everything," said the young man confidently.

When the young man had gone, Mrs McLetchie asked:

"How did you get on with him?"

"Well," said McLetchie, "the bad news is, he has no money, no job, and no prospects. On the other hand, he thinks I'm God."

Guide in Glasgow's Burrell Museum: "These Egyptian carvings are more than three thousand years old. Perhaps Moses saw them, when he was a boy."

Visitor: "I never knew Moses had been to Glasgow."

Our Minister is a true shepherd to his flock – we see it in every sermon he preaches on Sunday mornings: while we are slumbering, he is awake.

The minister was coming to tea, and wee Jamie had been warned to say nothing about the reverend's nose, which was somewhat large and red.

Everything was passing off very well, when the mother noticed that her little boy was staring rather hard at the minister. She gave him a disapproving look.

"It's alright, ma," he said loudly. "I wasn't going to say anything – I'm just looking at it."

An old man had died, and the young priest came to pay his last respects. The widow took him in to view the body. Trying hard to find something to say, he managed:

"He's got quite a tan, hasn't he? That last week at Troon must have done him a power of good."

"Jock and I have been discussing our future," said the elderly lady to her friend.

"When one of us dies, I'm going to go and live in Inverness."

"Now then, Miss McLeary," said the prosecuting counsel, "tell the court clearly – was it or was it not you that on the evening of August fourth did a strip tease in the High Street, mooned through the door of the McGreedy's public house at the men inside, hit a police officer with your shoe, climbed on top of his car, then jumped off it over the hedge of the bowling green, where you lay on your back shouting "Jack high"?

The woman thought deeply, then said:

"What date did you say again?"

"Why are you crying?" young Jimmy asked little Maisie next door.

"'Cos my my granny's gone to heaven," she sobbed.

"Och well, don't cry – maybe she hasn't," said Jimmy sympathetically.

A queue of people were waiting at the bus station in Edinburgh to get the bus to Portobello. When it finally pulled in, a man in line suddenly took out his glass eye and tossed it high in the air. Catching it expertly, he re-inserted it in place.

"What did you do that for?" gasped the woman behind him.

"I just wanted to see if there were places on the top deck."

On a bus, a middle-aged man sprang up promptly to give his seat to a lady who was standing.

"That was very gallant of you," said his wife as they got off.

"When I was a boy at school I learned to respect a woman with a strap in her hand," he replied.

When old Mr Abernethy reached the age of 100, a reporter from Radio Clyde came round to chat with him.

"And how do you feel when you wake up in the morning?" he asked.

"Increasingly surprised," replied Mr Abernethy.

After the election for the Scottish Parliament, as the political parties bargained over which policies would prevail in the coalition government, Mrs Broon complained to her husband:

"I don't like all this horse-trading."

"Perhaps it will result in a stable government," said Mr Broon.

"Well, I don't like being saddled with this lot, anyway," said Mrs Broon.

"They're just jockeying for position," said Mr Broon.

"Maybe we're taking a blinkered view," said Mrs Broon.

"We'll know when it comes to the bit," said Mr Broon.

"If only there was one without a head in the nose-bag," said Mrs Broon.

"There's a horse that won't run," said Mr Broon.

"I haven't spoken to my wife in 25 years."

"Good gracious! Why not?"

"She doesn't like being interrupted."

Back in the thirteenth century, Sir Angus Mac Cormack was planning to leave for war. Before setting off, he equipped his wife with a chastity belt, and entrusted the key to his best friend, Sir Simon de Bruce. Then he rode off, his mind at peace. He had almost reached the harbour when he noticed a horseman galloping at a furious rate behind him. When the rider caught him up, he was surprised to see that it was Sir Simon.

"You left the wrong key with me!" puffed Sir Simon.

The doctor in a village near Dumfries went off for a week's shooting in the Scottish Highlands. On his return, he dropped in at the local shop.

"Did you kill anything, doctor?" asked the shop-keeper.

He shook his head.

"Not a thing," he said. "We had rotten luck."

"Ach, you'd have done better staying at home and working," said the shopkeeper.

"Cheer up!" said his friend to the depressed Kennedy. "Why don't you drown your sorrows?"

Kennedy, a married man with three strapping daughters at home, turned a doleful face towards him and said:

"No man, that would be murder."

On the first night of yet another smart new restaurant in Glasgow's West End, a diner stared down at his artistically-arranged plate of minimalist fare, then looked across to his wife.

"Moira," he announced, "when I want food, I want food. When I want interior design, I hire a painter."

Big McTurk came into the bar one evening with his arm in plaster.

"What's the matter?" they asked.

"Broke my arm."

"But how?"

"I was fightin' for a woman's honour."

"Good for you, McTurk," they said.

"Aye," sighed McTurk, "she wanted to keep it."

When Mrs Broon appeared in her new fur coat, she was accosted by an angry animal lover.

"What poor creature had to die for you to get that fur coat?"

"If you really want to know, it was my mother-in-law," said Mrs Broon.

Mrs Kelvinside was displaying her diamond necklace, ruby bracelet and emerald brooch to her friend Mrs Morningside in the ladies' loo.

"How do you clean them?" asked Mrs Morningside. "I always use finest cognac to wash my diamonds. But I find the sapphires come out best if they're dipped in champagne."

"Oh, when mine are dirty I just throw them away," said Mrs Kelvinside.

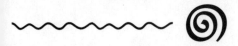

When her little boy came home from school crying, his mother was very concerned.

"What is it Fergus, has someone been hitting you?"

"No," he sobbed.

"Was the teacher cross with you?"

"No," he sobbed.

"What is it, then?"

"Kevin Carswell is flitting to Aberdeen."

"Oh, but there will still be plenty other little boys to play with."

He gave another sob.

"But he was the only one I could beat," he said.

How long does it take to tune a bagpipe?
We have yet to find out.

In the Sunday School class the teacher asked:
  "Who is it that knows everything we say and do?"
  "Mrs Hall next door, Miss," said one of her pupils.

After the big storm, a friend came out to visit Farmer Coupland.

"Did you have a lot of damage?"

"It was terrible," said the farmer. "The roof blew off the piggery, the walls fell down, the pigs that weren't squashed flat all ran away."

"Oh dear," said the friend. "And I hear Kerr's barn blew down, and his silo tower was knocked over and crashed through the roof of the house. Then the house caught fire and burned to the ground. And Johnston's milking parlour was flooded and all his machinery ruined. Half his cows were swept away when the river burst its banks. His whole farm is still under water."

"Ah well," said Farmer Coupland, brightening considerably. "There's some consolation there, after all."

The driver of a heavy truck, roaring at 70 miles an hour down the M8 from Edinburgh to Glasgow, was amazed to see a face appear at his side window. Winding it down hurriedly, he saw it was a motorcyclist, standing on the saddle of a powerful racing bike, controlling the handlebars with one foot. Shouting into the slipstream, he yelled to the truck driver:

"Have you got a light?"

"You'll kill yourself," called the driver, handing out his lighter.

"No, no," said the biker. "I only smoke three a day."

An English visitor to Glasgow was sitting in a pub in the East End, and after a few drinks began to feel he was getting into the swing of things. Turning to his neighbour, he said:

"What a terrible squint that barman has got."

The man glared back and said:

"Ye're talkin' about my cousin Charlie."

The visitor gulped.

"And doesn't it suit him well?" he said.

"Sir! Kindly leave the pool immediately!" called the attendant.

"What's wrong?" asked the man.

"You peed in it."

"Well, lots of people do that, don't they?"

"Not from the high diving board."

"I'd vote for the devil before I voted for you," shouted a heckler at the Parliamentary candidate.

"Yes, but what if your friend isn't standing?" replied the candidate.

In the Horseshoe Bar a card game was in progress, when all of a sudden a loud exclamation was heard.

"You old devil – you're cheating!"

"What do you mean, I'm cheating?"

"These aren't the cards I dealt you!"

"Did I step on your feet when I went out for the interval?"

"You most certainly did."

"See, Maggie, I told you this was the right row."

"My wife says you're an effeminate specimen."

"I suppose I am, compared to her."

"Fergus is such a pessimist. Even when there's light at the end of the tunnel he thinks it's an oncoming train."

A visitor to a Fife cemetery couldn't help noticing a man in one of the farther-off areas of the cemetery. He was kneeling in front of a gravestone, clasping his hands, and sobbing. The visitor went a bit closer. Presently he could hear what the man was saying.

"Why did you have to die?" he was repeating, brokenly. "Why did you have to die?"

Feeling he ought to do something, the visitor laid his hand on the man's shoulder.

"Was it someone you loved very much?" he asked, gently.

The man looked up at him.

"I never met him," he said. "He was my wife's first husband."

Hamish: How's your brother, Declan?
Declan: Oh, he's not been the same since his accident. They had to remove a third of his brain, you know. So we had him sent to England.
Hamish: To which hospital?
Declan: Who said anything about a hospital?

Whatever the Thomsons did, the next-door neighbours always seemed able to go one better. If the Thomsons went skiing in France, the Fergusons went to a more expensive resort in Switzerland. When the Thomsons bought a boat with an outboard motor, the Fergusons bought a motor launch. When the Thomsons had an open-air swimming pool installed, the Fergusons followed up with a climate-controlled indoor pool with jacuzzi and sauna. One day Mrs Thomson invited the neighbours for Sunday lunch, and put on her best show. At the start of the meal, she asked her little daughter, Jenny, to say grace. The child became tongue-tied.

"I don't know what to say," she muttered.

"Just say what you've heard mummy saying so many times," said her mother, encouragingly. "You know, Dear Lord—." The child immediately piped up:

"Dear Lord, what on earth was I thinking of, asking these wretched show-offy Fergusons to lunch?"

The tourist had been fishing for two weeks on Loch Lomond without even getting a bite. Then, on the last day, he finally hooked and landed a salmon. He looked at it a little wryly.

"You know, Tommy," he said to his gillie, "this fish has cost me six hundred dollars."

"Well, sir," said Thomas, "it's a good thing you only caught the one."

A lawyer was out for a day's shooting, and strayed away from the rest of the party. He had hit nothing all day, but as he turned to rejoin them, he suddenly saw a fine grouse flying close by. Instantly he brought up his gun and bang! – he got it. It fell to the ground at the other side of a fence, and as he leapt over to retrieve it, another man came running up.

"Hey!" he shouted. "This is my land."

"But it's my grouse," said the lawyer.

"No it's not. I saw you shooting over the fence."

"Listen, friend," said the lawyer. "I am a Glasgow lawyer specialising in property. You don't want to tangle with me or you'll find yourself in court, on the losing side, and facing the biggest bill for costs that you ever saw in your life. Get it?"

"I see," said the farmer. "Well, why don't we settle it country-style, man-to-man?"

"What do you mean?" asked the lawyer.

"It's a kick-and-yell contest," said the farmer. "We take turns to bend over and let the other fellow kick us. Six kicks a round. The first to yell is the loser."

"Okay," said the lawyer. He was a stout, burly fellow and the other looked a lightweight by comparison. He bent over. My God, he thought, but the man can kick! It was all he could do to stop himself yelling with the pain. After the sixth he stood up, his backside aching but his eyes gleaming for revenge, and saw the other man holding out the grouse.

"I've decided you can have it, after all," said the farmer, pleasantly.

"**M**y grandfather lived to ninety-five and never used glasses."

"Really? Drank straight from the bottle, I suppose?"

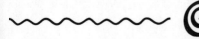

Two elderly ladies from Morningside went out for a drive one afternoon. Both of them had become a little vague with the passing of the years. They had intended to take quiet country roads, but took a couple of wrong turns and found themselves travelling into central Edinburgh. Mrs Coull, sitting in the passenger seat, noticed that Mrs Dunnet had driven through a red light. Then she did it again. Maybe I'm imagining it, thought Mrs Coull, and didn't say anything. Then it happened a third time. With a screech of brakes, a double decker bus just avoided them and crashed into a shop-front. The ladies proceeded on their way, at a gentle pace.

"Was that a red light, Mary?" asked Mrs Coull, hesitantly, at last.

"My goodness," said Mrs Dunnet, "am I driving?"

"**S**urely you're not going to drive that car," said the policeman, advancing on the motorist who had just emerged from the pub.

"Well, offisher, do you think I'm in any condition to walk?"

Barry Davie turned up late in the evening at one of his usual haunts.

"Have you seen Kevin McCrae?" he asked the barman.

"He was here about an hour ago."

Davie tried to focus his eyes on the barman.

"Was I with him?" he inquired.

A clothing shop in Aberdeen ordered a new consignment for the season, from its whole-saler. The message came back:

"Impossible to supply order until previous shipments paid for."

The owner replied:

"Please cancel the order; we cannot wait that long for delivery."

A dog-fancier's wife gave birth to triplets. The husband came to the hospital to see them but his mind was on other things. He looked the babies over critically, turned to the nurse and said:

"We'll keep the one in the middle."

"**D**o you remember young Ranald? He used to be terribly busy running around, trying to get a job from his friends in the Scottish Executive."

"Oh yes, what's he doing now?"

"Nothing – he got the job."

Mrs Hall was telling her next-door neighbour, Mrs Jamieson, the latest thing she had heard about the woman across the road.

"Tell me more," said Mrs Jamieson, fascinated.

"I can't," said Mrs Hall. "I've already told you more than I heard myself."

K_{eir}: "What kind of beer is this we're drinking?"

Weir: "Don't complain – you'll be old and weak yourself one day."

W_{aiting} in the line to get into the trendy new bar in Glasgow's Merchant City, big Senga became impatient.

"If they weren't so crowded, they'd do a lot better business," she muttered to her pal.

"W_{here} did you go for your holidays?"

"Tenerife."

"Where is Tenerife, anyway?"

"I don't know, we flew there."

Seeing that Shug was having some trouble opening his front door, a passing neighbour said: "Here, can I help you with that key?"

Swaying like a willow in a gale, Shug said:

"I could manage the key all right, but if you would jush maybe hold the house still for me . . ."

Two seasoned drinkers were rolling home one night. Down the road ahead of them they saw the bright lights of the big brewery.

"It's nice to know, isn't it," said one, "that no matter how much we drink, they're still ahead of us. They'll always make it faster than we can drink it."

"Maybe," said his friend, "but I see we have them working nights."

Having had a profitable year in his furniture store, Magnus, a bachelor, decided to celebrate by having a holiday in Paris. When he came back he met his friend Fergus.

"Were you not lonely there by yourself, and without a word of French?" asked Fergus.

"Not a bit," said Magnus. "I sat down in the park next to this girl. I drew a picture of a car, and she went for a taxi ride with me. I drew two glasses and we went to a café. I drew two plates and she showed me a very nice restaurant where we had a wonderful meal. After the meal she borrowed my pen and paper, and drew a big, wide bed. . ."

"Amazing," interrupted Fergus. "So she even could tell you were in the furniture business."

~~~~~~~~~~ ◎ ~~~~~~~~~~

An obscene caller from Aberdeen had a short career. He kept on reversing the charges.

~~~~~~~~~~ ◎ ~~~~~~~~~~

Pacing the floor of his general store, Mr Crombie was annoyed to hear one of his shop assistants say to a customer:

"No, we haven't had any this long while, and there's no sign of any coming, either."

When the customer had gone, he hurried over to berate the girl.

"I heard what you were saying," he hissed. "You're supposed to say, 'We haven't any just at the moment but we can order it for immediate delivery."

The girl looked bemused.

"We were talking about the rain," she said.

~~~~~~~~~~ ~~~~~~~~~~

After a slap-up meal in the town's best restaurant, Colquhoun called for a large brandy and a carton of washing-up liquid.

"Are you sure you want a carton of washing-up liquid, sir?" asked the waiter.

"Pretty sure," sighed Colquhoun. "You see, I don't actually have any money."

"**E**xcuse me," said Ina to her employer, "you're a pound short with my wages this week."

"You didn't complain last week when I paid you a pound too much," said the employer.

"I can overlook one mistake," said Ina.

"Do you believe in life after death?" said the office supervisor to Mr Ogg.

"I do indeed," said Mr Ogg.

"I'm glad to hear it," said the supervisor, "Because after you'd taken the day off yesterday to go to your Uncle John's funeral, I saw him walking down the road this morning."

"Good evening," said the man at the door. "I'm collecting for the school swimming pool. Would you like to contribute?"

"Certainly," said Shug. "Hold on a minute."

He went back into the house, then reappeared with a jug of water.

Mr Kelvinside was accustomed to giving his wife the best of everything. When she had to go into hospital for a minor operation, he came to speak to the surgeon.

"I'll just give her a local anaesthetic," said the surgeon.

"You'll do nothing of the kind," said Mr Kelvinside. "Spare no expense. Get one flown in."

"How's the mouth?" said the dentist, when Mr Dwyer came for his check-up.

"Oh, she's away seeing the sister," he replied.

At the wake held for a notorious troublemaker, a sudden silence fell. To break it, someone said:

"Who can say something good about Hamish?"

The silence deepened. Then at last one of the mourners spoke:

"His brother was worse," he said.

Being a financially prudent man, Mr Begbie was rather upset when he accidentally let a 50p piece fall into the public toilet.

"What shall I do?" he wondered. "Is it worth delving in there for 50p?" Then he had a brain-wave. Reaching into his pocket, he found another 50p piece, and dropped it in too.

"A pound's another matter entirely," he thought, rolling up his sleeve.

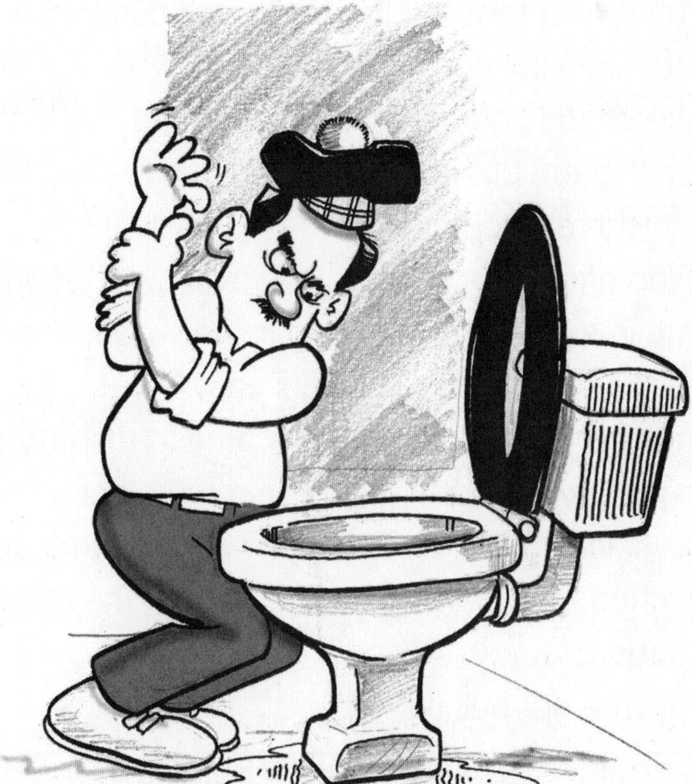

Two men were out for a stroll when they saw a third coming towards them. He was carrying a good-sized salmon.

"Where did you get that?" they asked.

"Back there at the bridge," he said.

But where's your rod?"

"Who needs a rod? Just lean over, wait for one to come in sight, put your hand in, very gently tickle its belly, then hook it out – it's easy."

They hurried on. When they came to the bridge it seemed rather high, so one held the other's ankles, letting him dangle over with his arms outstretched, and waited. Two hours later the other shouted:

"Pull me up, pull me up!"

"Have you caught something?" asked his friend.

"No," he cried, "but there's a train coming."

Big MacAngus was striding along one day
when he heard a cry for help, coming from a
peat bog. Looking into the distance, he saw a
man up to his shoulders in peat and moss.

"I'm coming!" shouted MacAngus, and hurried over as fast as he could whilst minding his
footing. The man had obviously sunk into a
particularly soft spot.

"Don't you worry, friend," said MacAngus,
"they don't call me Big MacAngus for nothing.
I'll soon hoist you out."

Bracing his feet against the ground, he put his
arms under the man's shoulders and heaved.
Nothing happened. He tried again. His own feet
began to sink in.

"This is really clinging stuff," he said. Just
then, he saw Muscles MacCosh walking by in
the distance, and called him over.

"You're in luck," he said. "MacCosh and me

are the two strongest men in the region. We'll soon have you out now."

The two mighty men tried to hoist the trapped man. But they could not move him. Slowly but surely, he was sinking in further. They exchanged anxious glances.

"He's going to be a goner," whispered MacCosh. The sinking man overheard him.

"Would it maybe help if I took my feet out of the stirrups?" he asked.

A visiting Texan aroused the attention of the regulars in a Scottish pub when he announced a bet.

"You may say the Scots are powerful drinkers, but I'll bet five hundred dollars there's not a man here who can drink ten pints of beer in a row."

He gazed round, challengingly. But none of them responded to his challenge. One man even got to his feet and silently left the place. The Texan

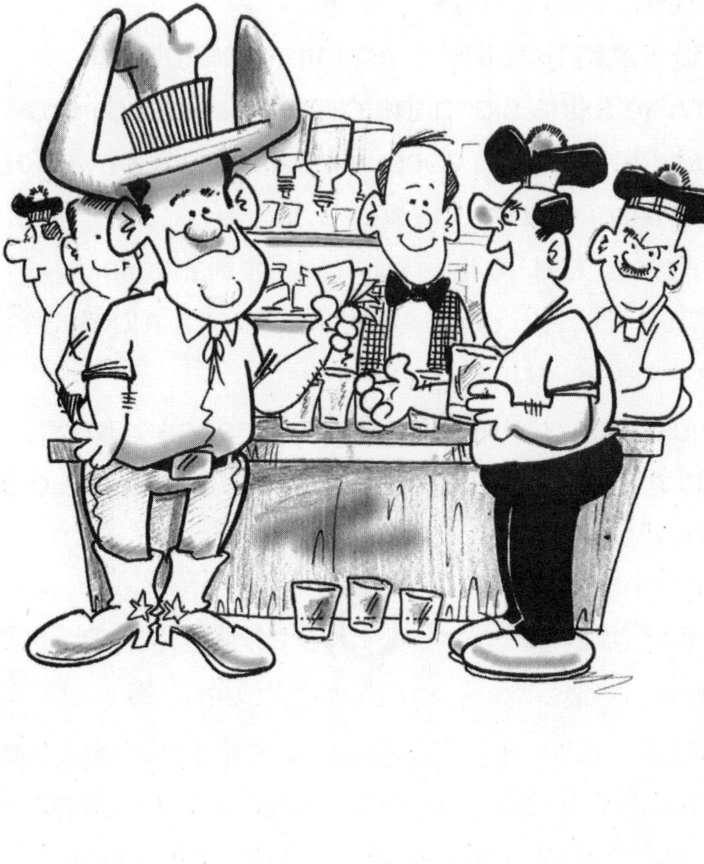

shrugged and sipped at his own drink. A few minutes later he felt a tap on his shoulder, and looked round. The man who had gone out had come back.

"Is your bet still on?"

"Sure."

The Texan had the barman lay ten full pints of heavy in a line along the counter. In steady progression, the man consumed them all, leaving ten foam-lined empty glasses. There was a ripple of applause. The Texan reached for his wallet.

"What did you go out for, if it's not a rude question?" he asked.

"I just went to the pub across the road, to check that I really could drink ten pints in a row," said the man.